T0150700

RECYCLED
Craft Projects
FOR KIDS

RECYCLED
Craft Projects
FOR KIDS

50 fantastic things to make from junk, shown step by step
in over 400 photographs

MARION ELLIOT

ARMADILLO

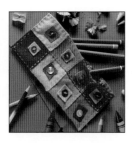

The author would like to thank Joanne Rippin; John Freeman and Adrian Cole for the photography; Susan Bull for her styling; and Neil Hadfield for his design and technical expertise and encouragement.

The author and publishers would also like to thank Noah Goodrich, Anya Rupesinghe, Nicholas Staib, Alice Summers and Nicholas Watkins from Prospect House School, Putney, London, for appearing in the photographs.

This edition is published by Armadillo, an imprint of Anness Publishing Ltd, Blaby Road, Wigston, Leicestershire LE18 4SE; info@anness.com

www.annesspublishing.com

If you like the images in this book and would like to investigate using them for publishing, promotions or advertising, please visit our website www.practicalpictures.com for more information.

© Anness Publishing Ltd 2013

Publisher: Joanna Lorenz
Project Editor: Joanne Rippin
Photographer: John Freeman
Designers: Adrian Morris and Lucy Doncaster
Stylist: Susan Bull
Production Controller: Mai-Ling Collyer

SAFETY NOTE
• Crafts and hobbies are great fun to learn and can fill hours of rewarding leisure time, but some points should be remembered for safety and care of the environment.
• Always choose non-toxic materials wherever possible – for example, paint, glue and varnishes. Where these are not suitable use materials in a well-ventilated area and always follow manufacturers' instructions.
• Needles, scissors and all sharp tools should be handled with care. Always use a cutting board or mat to avoid damage to surfaces.
• Protect surfaces from paint and glue splashes with newspapers.
• Although the advice and information in this book are believed to be accurate and true at the time of going to press, neither the authors nor the publisher can accept any legal responsibility or liability for any errors or omissions that may have been made nor for any inaccuracies nor for any loss, harm or injury that comes about from following instructions or advice in this book.

Manufacturer: Anness Publishing Ltd, Blaby Road, Wigston, Leicestershire LE18 4SE, England
For Product Tracking go to: www.annesspublishing.com/tracking
Batch: 6829-22584-1127

CONTENTS

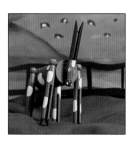

INTRODUCTION

Just think of all the different things we all throw away without a second thought! It is estimated that we produce several times our own weight in rubbish every year. We haven't even used some of the things that we dispose of, because they are used to package our everyday items, such as food, drinks, soap powder, toothpaste and washing-up detergent.

Instead of wasting all these pieces of plastic, paper and cardboard, it is much better to make them into something new, such as the fun toys, games, adornments and decorations that are in this book. All the projects are made using things that you might throw away every day and the best news is that most of the materials are free. You will be able to make a lot of the projects by yourself, but you will need adult help for some of them, so be sure to ask when the project says to do so. Don't worry if you can't find exactly the same materials to recycle as appear in each project; the best bit about using packaging is that there is so much to choose from that you can pick the materials that you like the best!

Recycling

This book shows you lots and lots of exciting ways to use waste materials to make fun projects. Once you have started to collect junk, you will realize just how much packaging, newspaper, cardboard and plastic we all throw away every day.

If we take the trouble to put old bottles, newspapers and cans in special banks, they can be made into new ones. This helps to use the earth's resources more wisely.

Apart from recycling your household waste in special banks, you can also re-use it to make lots of exciting things. Before you throw something away, look at it carefully and ask yourself a few questions. Is it an interesting shape or a nice shade? Does it suggest an idea for a project to you? Can you think of an ingenious way of making it into something new and completely different? If the answer to any of these is yes, hang on to it and start a collection of interesting materials. Here are some of the things to look out for.

Cardboard tubes and rolls
These can be found in the middle of rolls of foil, toilet paper and adhesive tape. They are also used to protect rolled paper. Tubes are great for making models, such as telescopes, and for creating any number of junk sculptures.

Cord, sewing thread and string in various shades
This is good for stringing beads, making mobiles, joining sections of models and puppets, and hanging decorations. Collect discarded scraps from parcels and packages.

Corrugated cardboard
This is great for making models, frames and adornments. Corrugated cardboard comes in different thicknesses and can be one or more layers deep. Keep your eyes open for discarded TV and computer boxes when you are out because they are a great source of good-quality cardboard.

Elastic bands
These stretchy bands come in lots of different shades and sizes. Some are very thin and springy, which are the kind you need for projects such as the pinball machine. Others are thicker and stronger, and are helpful for holding a project together while the glue dries.

Fabric scraps
Material can be quite expensive to buy and you will usually only need a little bit for each project. If you know anyone who sews, ask them to keep scraps for you.

Newspapers
We throw away tons and tons of newspaper every day. It comes in all sorts of different shades, thicknesses and sizes. It is very good for making papier-mâché, folding into hats and covering your work surface.

Plastic bags
Some bags are bright and are good for making puppets' clothes. They are also good for keeping your collection of materials tidy! Plastic bags can be very dangerous, so you must never leave them where babies and young children might find them.

Plastic bottles
These come in lots of different shapes and sizes and can be various bright shades or clear. They are good for making musical instruments and toys such as puppets and skittles.

Paper clips (fasteners)
These clips come in lots of different sizes and shades. They are good for decorating junk sculptures, especially robots, and are useful for holding projects together while the glue dries.

Plastic food containers
These come in many interesting shapes and some are very decorative. They make great bases for papier-mâché and are also good for adding details to large models, such as astronauts or space stations.

From left to right, top row: *cardboard tubes and rolls, cord, sewing thread and string in various shades, corrugated cardboard, elastic bands.* Middle row: *paper clips, fabric scraps, scrap paper, plastic food containers.* Bottom row: *newspapers, plastic bags, plastic bottles.*

Materials and Equipment

These are just some of the materials used in this book. Some you will already have, others you may have to buy.

Adhesive tape
This can be used for sticking paper, cardboard and foil.

Bright adhesive dots
These come in a variety of shades and sizes and are available from most stationers.

Cardboard tubes
These come in a variety of sizes in the centres of toilet rolls, kitchen-paper rolls and rolls of foil.

Cord
This is very strong and is good for necklaces and hanging mobiles.

Corks
Corks are good for making small dolls, animals and other toys.

Darning needles
These are wide needles with large eyes and rounded ends that are not very sharp. Use them for sewing, for stringing beads and for threading elastic.

Elastic bands
These come in lots of shades and different lengths.

Elastic
It is possible to buy thin elastic in many different shades.

Fabric and felt scraps
Scraps of fabric and felt are useful for making fabric pictures, toys' clothes and patchwork. Felt comes in lots of shades and doesn't fray.

Felt-tipped pens
Available in a huge range of shades and thicknesses, these are used for decorating paper and cardboard. They must be non-toxic.

Masking tape
This tape is made from paper and is easy to peel off objects.

Measuring tape
You sometimes need this for measuring fabric.

Natural objects
These can be picked up in parks and during country walks. Always show an adult before you use it, to make sure that it is safe.

Paintbrushes
These come in a variety of sizes. Use a medium-thick brush for general painting and for applying glue. Use fine brushes to paint more detailed designs.

Paints
These must be non-toxic. Poster paints are good because they come in lots of lovely shades.

Palette
Use this useful container for holding paint. Alternatively, an old saucer or carton can be used and is just as good.

Paper glue
This must be non-toxic and comes in liquid form, which can be spread with a special spreader or a solid stick. The liquid form is best for models, while the solid type is best for sticking paper together.

Pencils
A soft pencil is useful for making tracings and transferring them to cardboard and paper.

White glue
This must be non-toxic. It is very sticky and is good for gluing cardboard and fabric. It can also be mixed with poster paints to make them stick to plastic surfaces. It is useful as a varnish and, if you dilute it, you can use it to make papier-mâché.

Ruler
A ruler is useful for measuring and drawing straight lines.

Scissors
These should be of the type that are made specially for children and have rounded blades.

Sewing thread
This comes in lots of bright shades and thicknesses and is good for patchwork and sewing.

Silver and bright foil
This comes on long rolls and is good for making jewels and mirrors.

Strong glue
This must be non-toxic and solvent-free. Strong glue is useful for sticking heavy cardboard and holding awkward joints together.

bright adhesive dots

bright fo

confectionery wrappers

corks

silver foil

white glue

palette

paper glue

paintbrushes

fabric scraps

paints

strong glue

felt-tipped pens

pencils

wooden spoons

ruler

scissors

natural objects

cardboard tubes

adhesive tape

cord and sewing threads

masking tape

elastic bands

darning needles

dressmaker's pins

paper clips

TECHNIQUES

Tracing

Some of the projects in this book have patterns that you can transfer directly to paper or use to make templates. Tracing is the quickest way to make copies of a pattern so that you can easily transfer it to another piece of paper or cardboard.

1 Lay your piece of tracing paper on the pattern and use a soft pencil to draw over the image, making a dark line. Turn the sheet of tracing paper over and place it on a scrap of paper. Scribble over the lines with your pencil.

2 Turn the tracing right-side up again and place it on an appropriate piece of paper or cardboard. Carefully draw over the lines, pressing qute hard, to transfer the tracing to the paper or cardboard positioned underneath.

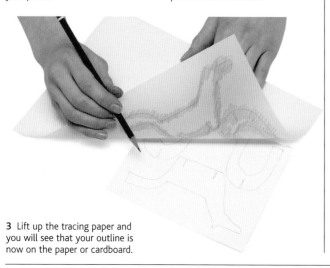

3 Lift up the tracing paper and you will see that your outline is now on the paper or cardboard.

Scaling-up

Sometimes you will want to make a project bigger than the template given. It's easy to make it larger. This is known as scaling-up. Use a scale of, say, one square on the template to two squares on the graph paper.

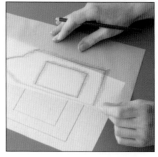 

1 If you wish to copy a template that is not printed on a grid, trace it as already described and transfer it to a piece of graph paper. If the template you have chosen does appear on a grid, proceed directly to step 2.

2 Using an appropriate scale, enlarge the template on to a second piece of paper, copying the shape from each smaller square to the larger square. Refer back regularly to the original drawing and try to match it as closely as you can.

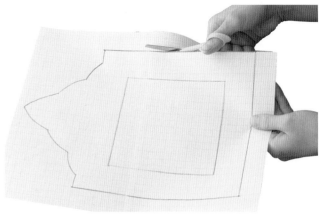

3 Cut out the template and transfer it to cardboard or paper.

Papier-mâché

Papier-mâché is made by shredding paper, usually old newspapers, and combining it with glue. The paper can be used in a number of ways to make a huge variety of objects that are either useful or just for decoration.

1 For most projects, paper should be torn into fairly short strips about 2cm (¾in) wide.

2 Mix some non-toxic white glue with water to the consistency of whipping cream.

3 Papier-mâché can be pressed into lightly greased forms or wrapped around cardboard shapes, as shown.

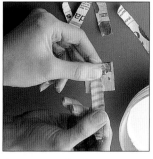

4 To cover smaller shapes, use small, thin pieces of newspaper, which are easier to position.

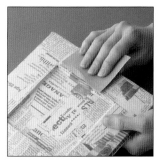

5 Your papier-mâché object may have a slightly rough surface when it has dried out. To make it uniformly smooth, lightly rub the surafce with fine abrasive paper.

6 Prime your papier-mâché with two coats of non-toxic white paint to conceal the newsprint surface before decorating.

Printing with Foam Rubber Stamps

Simple stamps can be cut from sheets of thin foam rubber and stuck on to cardboard bases. Use these recycled stamps to make your own special greetings cards, or even to decorate your walls.

1 To make the stamps, cut several rectangles of heavy cardboard measuring 5 x 6cm (2 x 2¼in). Cut an equal number of smaller rectangles measuring 1.5 x 6cm (⅝ x 2¼in) to form the handles. Stick the handles to the tops of the bases with strong glue.

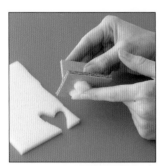

2 Draw the stamp motif on to foam rubber. Cut it out with scissors and glue it to the cardboard base. Allow to dry thoroughly.

3 Mix paint with water to a stiff consistency. Dip the stamp in the paint, then press it on to medium-weight paper or thin cardboard.

Painting on Plastic

All the projects in this book involve recycling and some are made from plastic bottles and yogurt cartons. Sometimes you may want to paint these, but ordinary poster paint will not stick to plastic. However, if you add glue to the paint it will be sticky and will cover the plastic well.

1 Put some ordinary poster paint in your chosen shade into a palette or small dish.

2 Pour in a little white glue. Carefully mix the paint and the glue, until they are mixed together.

3 Wash your plastic bottle in warm soapy water and dry thoroughly. Apply the paint mixture over the surface of the bottle, taking care to spread the paint smoothly. Wash your brush thoroughly, as soon as you have finished.

Flattening and Cutting Up a Box

Cardboard can be used for papier-mâché frames, among other things. Old boxes are the best source, and you can flatten them out easily.

1 Remove any tape that is holding the box together and press it flat.

2 Cut the box into pieces, ready for use in your various projects.

Removing a Label from a Bottle

Plastic bottles can be used for all kinds of projects. You will need to wash them thoroughly before using them or they may start to smell or even go mouldy.

1 Fill a washing-up bowl with warm soapy water.

2 Soak the bottle in the water for about ten minutes.

Re-using Foil Wrappers

Bright foil is great for decorations, and you don't have to buy it specially. Save old confectionery and cookie wrappers and cases made of pretty shades of foil, and cut them into different shapes, as required.

1 Flatten the wrappers and cases and smooth them out. Cut them up for use in your projects.

3 Peel the label off the bottle. If the label is still sticking to the bottle, soak it in the water for a little longer.

QUICK AND EASY IDEAS

COAT-HANGER TRIANGLE

If you want to make a triangle quickly, all you need is a metal coat-hanger, a teaspoon and a length of ribbon. The coat-hanger will make a pleasant, clear sound when you strike it and you could make even several triangles for your friends and form a small band!

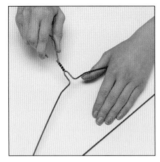

1 Ask an adult to bend over the hook of a metal coat-hanger, to create a closed loop at the top.

2 Cut a length of ribbon or cord and tie it around the loop. Tie the ends together to make a loop for holding.

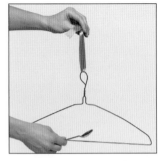

3 Hold your triangle in one hand and strike it with a metal teaspoon, to make a chiming sound.

WOODEN SPOON PUPPET

This is a quick and easy way to make a puppet. All you need is a wooden spoon, a plastic bag and some felt-tipped pens. However, don't give the puppet to young children, because plastic bags can be dangerous.

1 Lay a bright plastic carrier bag flat on a work surface. Snip off one bottom corner of the bag with scissors to make a small hole that the spoon handle will fit through.

2 Push the handle of a wooden spoon through the hole into the bag, as far as it will go. Tape the edges of the bag around the top of the spoon to keep the bag in place.

3 Using felt-tipped pens, draw your puppet's face on the front of the spoon. You can also draw buttons or patterns on the front of the bag to make the puppet's body more interesting, if you like.

LITTLE SHAKER

It is easy to make a percussion instrument that is small enough to fit in your hand.

This one is made from two bright yogurt pots, filled with dried rice.

MAKING FOIL BEADS

You can squash pieces of foil, roll them into balls, then glue them to things to make

decorations. Or you can cut thin strips and roll them up, to make long, thin beads.

1 Wash and dry the yogurt pots thoroughly. Pour a small handful of rice into one of them.

2 Spread a little glue around the tops of the yogurt pots. Place the second yogurt pot on top of the first and press the two pots firmly together. Let the glue dry thoroughly before you try to play your shaker.

1 Squash and roll scraps of foil into little balls, to make small round beads. Press one side of each bead to make a flat surface, so that you can glue them to all manner of things as decoration.

2 To make long, thin beads, cut a piece of foil into strips 2.5cm (1in) wide. Lay a pencil at one end of a strip and roll the strip around the pencil, to make a tube. Tape the ends together, to stop it unravelling.

QUICK PAPER BAG MASK

If you want a mask quickly you can make a good one from a large brown paper bag. You must never make one from a plastic carrier bag, though, as they are very dangerous. Before you start, make sure the bag is not too small for your head, or so big that you get lost in it and it keeps falling off.

1 Draw three holes on the front of the mask and cut them out to make openings for your eyes and mouth.

2 Roll up the bottom of the paper bag two or three times, so that it comes down just past your chin. Twist the top corners to make ears for the mask.

3 Decorate both the front and back of your mask, using felt-tipped pens, glitter, foil or whatever takes your fancy, to create your own unique and exciting design.

TEMPLATES

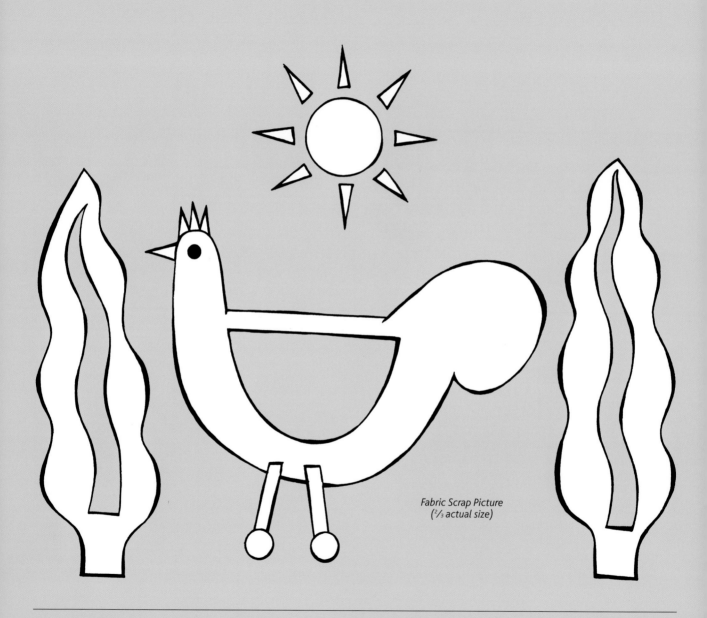

Fabric Scrap Picture
(⅔ actual size)

Sponge-flower Hair Band
(actual size)

Storage Chest
(actual size)

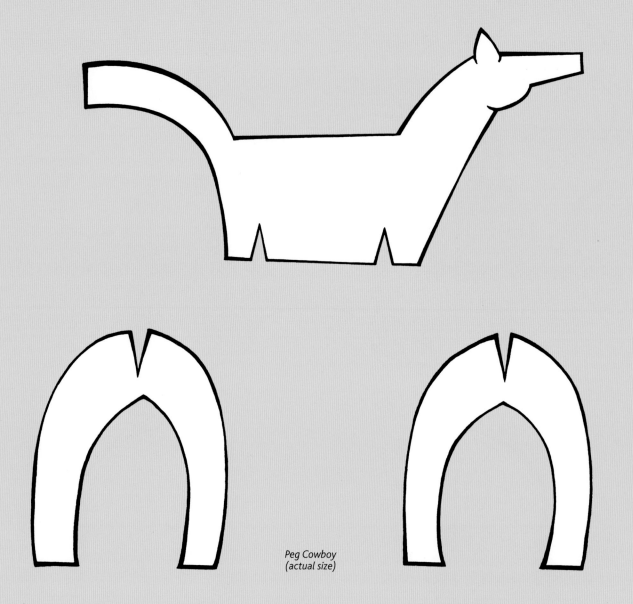

Peg Cowboy
(actual size)

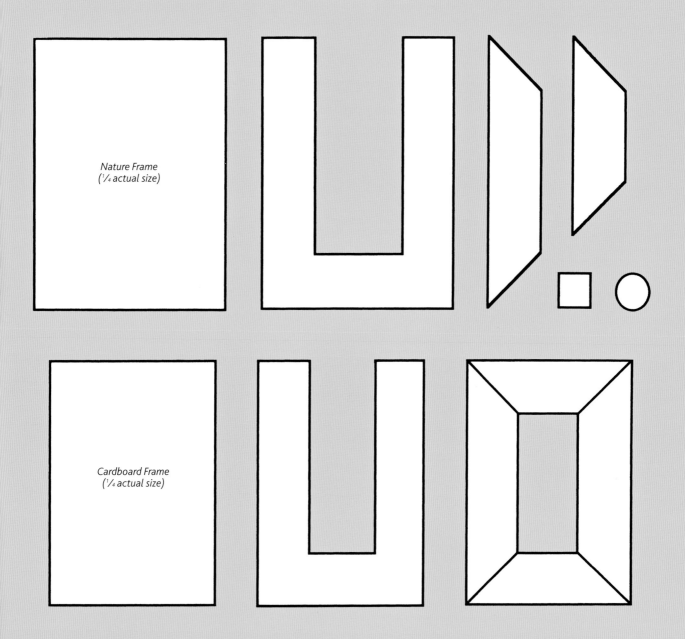

Nature Frame
(¼ actual size)

Cardboard Frame
(¼ actual size)

Junk Robot

All you need to make this fabulous robot is a large box, a plastic cup, some washing line, washing-up sponges and cardboard tubes. Its features and control panel are added with various odds and ends, such as bottle tops, yogurt pots and a safety pin, so keep an eye on the kitchen bin for useful robot parts!

RECYCLING TIP
Kitchen foil can be used more than once. If it has been used for food carefully wash it with soapy water and a sponge and then leave it to dry completely before re-using it.

YOU WILL NEED
white glue
4 cardboard tubes
washing line
elastic bands
plastic cup
kitchen foil
scissors
adhesive tape
washing-powder box
washing-up sponges
2 small yogurt pots
2 thick sponge scourers
3 round plastic scourers
bottle caps and other
    odds and ends
2 metal washers
safety pin
foil pie dishes

cardboard tubes

washing-up sponge

plastic scourer

foil pie dishes

adhesive tape

1 Put glue on the tops and bottoms of the tubes. Wrap washing line around the tubes. Hold it in place with elastic bands while the glue dries. Repeat with the plastic cup.

2 Cut a piece of kitchen foil that is large enough to cover the washing-powder box. Loosely crumple the foil, to give it a crinkly surface, and tape it around the box.

3 Cut two circles from washing-up sponge and glue them to one end of two of the tubes. Glue a small yogurt pot to the other end of both tubes to make the robot's arms.

4 To make the robot's legs, glue a thicker scourer to one end of the two remaining cardboard tubes. Stretch a round plastic scourer over each end of the tubes.

5 Glue bottle caps and other odds and ends to the front to make the controls. Glue two metal washers and a safety pin to the front of the plastic cup to make the robot's face.

6 Glue the cup to the top and put a plastic scourer over it to make the neck. Glue the legs to the bottom and one arm to each side; hold in place with elastic bands until the glue dries.

Wild West Ranch

Every cowboy needs a ranch and here's one to be proud of. The ranch house is a cardboard box covered with pieces of corrugated cardboard, which go well with the lolly stick roof and make the house look as if it's made from wood. The floor is made from coarse abrasive paper.

YOU WILL NEED
ruler
scissors
corrugated cardboard
strong, non-toxic glue
cardboard box
brown and green poster paints
paintbrush
paint-mixing container
thin cardboard
adhesive tape
lolly sticks
paper in various shades
coarse abrasive paper sheet

corrugated cardboard

scissors

adhesive tape

lolly sticks

paintbrush

poster paints

glue

pencil

ruler

1 Cut four pieces of corrugated cardboard to fit over the sides of the box, then glue them in place. Paint the cardboard brown, to look like wood.

2 To make the roof, cut two pieces of thin cardboard just longer than the length of the box. Tape them together on the back, so they fold in a roof shape. Glue lolly sticks to cover both sides of the roof on either side of the fold.

3 Cut a rectangle of thin cardboard as long as the top of the box and 5cm (2in) wider. Fold over 2.5cm (1in) on either side to make flaps. Glue the cardboard inside the roof to make a base. Glue the roof to the house.

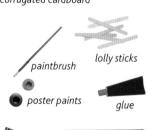

4 For windows, cut two squares of yellow paper; fold in four and cut a square out of the corner. Open out and glue on. Cut a rectangle of corrugated cardboard for a door.

5 Cut a rectangle of corrugated cardboard the same size as the abrasive paper sheet. Glue the sheet of abrasive paper to the cardboard and leave to dry.

6 To make the fence, cut a strip of corrugated cardboard 2.5cm (1in) high and long enough to fit all the way around the base. Glue in place and paint green.

Cowboys

These cowboys are ready to ride the range on their dappled horses. They are made from old-fashioned wooden pegs and look very smart in their gingham shirts and spotted neckerchiefs. The horses are made from thin cardboard and they can stand upright.

YOU WILL NEED

white, dark blue and red
  poster paints
paintbrushes
paint-mixing container
wooden clothes pegs (pins)
scissors
yellow, red and white
  paper scraps
strong, non-toxic glue
tracing paper
pencil
thin white cardboard
felt-tipped pens

wooden clothes peg

poster paints *scissors*

felt-tipped pen *pencil*

paintbrushes

paper scraps *glue*

1 Paint the top of a peg white. Paint the bottom half dark blue to make the cowboy's jeans.

2 When the first coat of paint has dried, add details, such as the cowboy's face and the checks on his shirt, using poster paints.

3 Cut a hat from yellow paper. Fold up the edges and then glue the hat to the front of the cowboy's head. Cut a neckerchief from red paper and add spots with white paint. Glue the neckerchief around the cowboy's neck.

4 Cut two strips of white paper to make the cowboy's arms. Paint a hand at the end of each strip and add checks. Glue the arms to the cowboy's sides.

5 Trace the horse patterns from the front of the book. Lay the tracings face-down on thin white cardboard and draw over the lines to transfer to the cardboard. Cut out all the pieces.

6 Using felt-tipped pens, draw in the horse's face and the markings on its body. Push the body into the slots in its legs. Sit the cowboy on his horse.

Space Station

If you like the idea of space travel, why not make yourself a floating space station like this one? It has a radar dish and a landing stage for you to park rockets and other spacecraft on. Look around for any interestingly-shaped odds and ends that would look good on your space station; paint them silver, and start building!

RECYCLING TIP
You can use different-sized boxes but make sure the cardboard isn't too thick, because if the boxes are very heavy the glue might not hold them together.

YOU WILL NEED
small and large
  cardboard boxes
paintbrush
paint-mixing container
silver poster paint
white glue
4 paper bowls
cardboard tubes
2 round foil pie dishes
strong, non-toxic glue
2 yogurt pots
drinking straw
round cardboard carton
rectangular foil dish

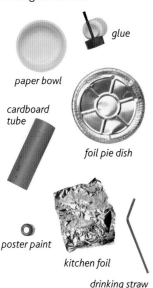

glue

paper bowl

cardboard tube

foil pie dish

poster paint

kitchen foil

drinking straw

1 Paint the large cardboard box and the smaller one silver. You may have to paint the boxes twice to cover the cardboard properly with no cardboard showing through. Leave to dry completely.

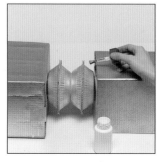

2 Glue the rims of two paper bowls together with white glue. Glue two more in the same way. Stick all four together. Paint them silver and glue them between the two boxes to make an airlock.

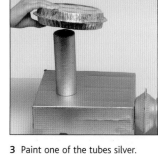

3 Paint one of the tubes silver. Glue the rims of the foil pie dishes together with strong glue; glue them to the top of the tube. Stick the tube to the larger box to make a landing stage.

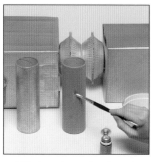

4 Add white glue to the silver paint. Paint the yogurt pots, one small and two large cardboard tubes silver. Glue one pot to the small tube. Stick this next to the landing pad.

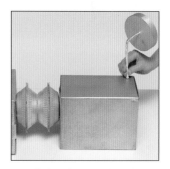

5 Stick the tubes on either side of the pot to the end. Cover the straw with foil and paint the round carton silver. Join together and stick to the smaller box.

6 Stick the rectangular foil dish upside-down next to the aerial.

Tanker Truck

Collect different sizes of cardboard boxes and see which look most like a truck when they are put together.

YOU WILL NEED
4 long, thin cotton reels (spools)
4 small jar lids
strong, non-toxic glue
drinking straws
scissors
thin cardboard scraps
square and rectangular
  cardboard boxes
2 short cotton reels (spools)
squeezy bottle
white paper
yellow, blue and red
  poster paints
paintbrushes
paint-mixing container

paintbrush

drinking straws

cardboard   *squeezy bottle*

glue

cotton reels

poster paints

jar lids

1 Glue a cotton reel to the middle of the inside of each jar lid, or the wheels. Cut two lengths of straw about 4cm (1½in) longer than the widths of the cabin and trailer boxes to make axles. Glue each axle inside one of the cotton reels at each end.

2 Cut four strips of cardboard measuring 5 x 1.5cm (2 x ½in). Bend each strip into a U shape. Spread glue on one end and attach two to the bottom of the cabin and two to the bottom of the trailer. Place a pair of wheels inside each U shape. Glue the open side of the other end in place.

3 Glue the two short cotton reels to the back of the cabin. Spread glue on the other end and stick the trailer to them. Leave the glue to dry completely. This may take about 30 minutes or even longer.

4 Glue a piece of white paper around the plastic squeezy bottle. Glue the bottle to the top of the trailer to make a tanker. Leave to dry completely. Decorate using poster paints.

Tin-can Stilts

Make a pair of these tin-can stilts and you'll be walking tall! Use very strong tin cans that can support your weight and choose those with removable lids, because they don't have a sharp rim. Ask an adult to file the edges of the holes smooth after they are punched, so they don't cut through the cord handles.

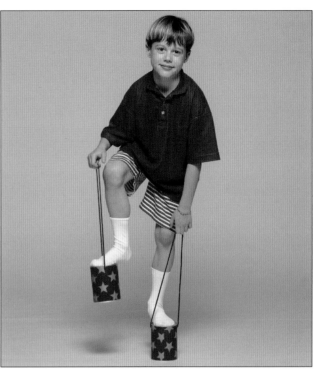

YOU WILL NEED
ruler
pencil
gift wrap
scissors
paper glue
2 strong tin cans, with
  removable lids
thick cord in a bright shade
adhesive tape

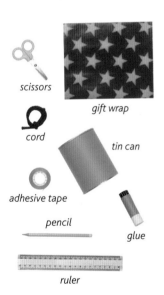

scissors

gift wrap

cord

tin can

adhesive tape

pencil

glue

ruler

1 Measure and draw out two strips of gift wrap, the same width as the cans and long enough to fit around them. Cut out the strips.

2 Glue one paper strip around each can. Ask an adult to punch a hole in each side of the unopened end of each can, near the rim. Ask the adult to file the edges of the holes completely smooth.

3 Cut two lengths of cord that are two-and-a-half times as long as the distance from your ankle to your knee. To make the handles, push the ends of the cords through the holes from the outside of the cans.

4 Tie a knot in the end of each handle to stop them pulling out of the holes. If the handles are the right length, tie an extra knot in the other end to keep them in place. If not, adjust the cord until they feel right.

Indoor Snowstorm

If you've saved some Christmas cake decorations and don't know what to do with them in the new year, why not use them to make a snowstorm? Glue them inside a clear plastic jar, add some water and a handful of glitter and you'll have a winter scene to remind you of Christmas. Make sure the jar lid fits tightly, so there's no chance of any of the water leaking out.

YOU WILL NEED
clear plastic jar, with lid
pencil
kitchen foil
scissors
strong, non-toxic glue
Christmas cake decorations,
    such as Santa Claus, reindeer
    and Christmas tree
water
gold glitter

water

scissors

kitchen foil

gold glitter

glue

Christmas cake decorations

1 Wash and dry the jar. Draw around the neck of the jar on a piece of foil. Cut out the circle of foil and glue it to the inside of the lid.

2 Glue Santa Claus, the reindeer and the Christmas tree to the lid and leave in a safe place for the glue to dry thoroughly overnight.

3 Fill the jar almost to the top with water. Carefully pour one heaped teaspoon of gold glitter into the water and stir it in.

4 Spread glue around the neck of the jar. Lower the decorations into the jar and screw the lid in place. When the lid is secure, turn the jar upside-down and shake it to see the snowstorm.

Paper-plate Cat Mask

Paper plates are great for making masks. You can either use them flat and cut holes for your eyes and mouth, or be a bit more ingenious and cut them to sit on your head.

YOU WILL NEED
pencil
paper plate
scissors
orange, blue, red and yellow
    poster paints
paintbrushes
paint-mixing container

paper plate

scissors

paintbrushes

*poster
paints*

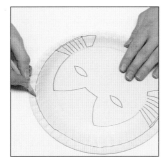

1 Using the pencil, carefully draw the mask design on the back of the paper plate.

2 Cut out the mask. Ask an adult to cut out the eye holes for you.

3 Paint the cat's face orange. Paint its collar blue, leaving four white dots to fill in later.

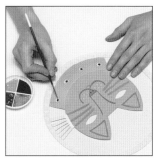

4 When the first coat of paint has dried, paint the cat's features on top and finish the collar.

Paper-bag Animal Mask

Plain paper bags are great for making masks quickly and easily. You can cut them into all sorts of different shapes and use felt-tipped pens to add exciting decoration. Collect brown-paper carrier bags to make masks too – they're stronger than standard paper bags and will last longer.

YOU WILL NEED
pencil
2 large paper bags
scissors
paper glue
orange, red and black
 felt-tipped pens

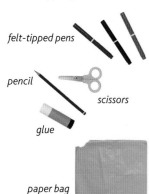

felt-tipped pens

pencil

scissors

glue

paper bag

1 Draw three holes on the front of your paper bag, for your eyes and mouth. Cut out the holes.

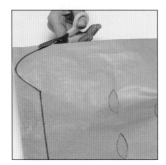

2 Draw two ears along the top edge of the bag and cut them out. Glue the top edges of the bag together again.

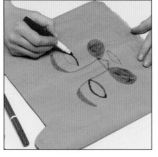

3 Carefully draw the animal's face on the front of the bag, using felt-tipped pens. Use the picture shown here as a guide, or create your own design. Draw red lines around the eyes so that they stand out.

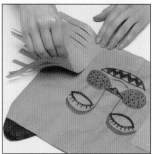

4 Cut three wide strips from another paper bag. Make long cuts along one long edge of each strip. Glue the uncut edges of the strips to the sides and top of the animal's head to make a mane.

Radical Robot

This robot is made from cotton reels and foil pie dishes.
Cotton reels are great because the hole in the middle means
they can easily be threaded together.

YOU WILL NEED
scissors
kitchen foil
17 small cotton reels (spools)
1 large cotton reel
adhesive tape
darning needle
thin elastic
4 small foil pie dishes
paper clips (fasteners)
press studs (snap fasteners)
strong, non-toxic glue

glue

paper clips

kitchen foil

press studs

scissors

foil pie dishes

cotton reels

1 Cut strips of kitchen foil about 1.5cm (½in) wider than the reels and long enough to fit around them. Cover the reels with foil.

2 To make the lower body, thread a darning needle with elastic and tie a big knot in the end. Ask an adult to make a hole in the middle of two dishes and two holes in a third. Thread a dish on to the elastic; then three small reels; then the dish with two holes; then three reels; then a dish. Tie a knot in the end and cut the elastic.

3 Ask an adult to make a hole in the middle of the last foil pie dish. To make the upper body, tie a knot in the end of a piece of elastic; thread on three small reels and a large reel for the head. Secure with a paper clip.

4 To make an arm, tie a paper clip to the end of some elastic, thread on four small reels and tie a knot in the end. Glue the dishes together and attach the arms below the head. Use paper clips and press studs for its face and controls.

Space Cat

Greetings, earthlings! Collect small yogurt cartons to make this fun, spotted space cat. Its legs are made from drinking straws and it stands on flat button feet. Try to find a suitable bottle cap like this one for its head, which has small points at the top that look just like ears.

RECYCLING TIP
Make sure you wash the yogurt cartons thoroughly in warm soapy water before you use them.

YOU WILL NEED
drinking straws
ruler
scissors
thin elastic
buttons
wooden beads
2 small yogurt cartons
strong, non-toxic glue
bright adhesive dots
bottle cap
black felt-tipped pen

bright adhesive dots

glue

felt-tipped pen

thin elastic

yogurt pots

drinking straw

buttons

bottle cap

wooden beads

1 Cut four pieces of drinking straw measuring 6cm (2in) long. Cut four pieces of thin elastic measuring 30cm (12in) long.

2 To make a leg, thread a piece of elastic through both holes in a button. Push the button to the middle of the elastic. Hold the ends together and thread on a wooden bead and a piece of straw. Repeat for the other legs.

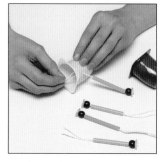

3 Ask an adult to make a hole in both sides of the cartons and in the end of one of them. Attach the legs to the cartons by pushing the ends of the elastic through the holes in the sides and tying them tightly.

4 To make the tail, thread a button, a bead and a 2cm (1in) piece of straw on to a 20cm (8in) length of elastic. Push the ends through the hole in the carton and knot tightly.

5 Spread glue along the top edges of both the cartons and stick them together. Leave the glue to dry. Add bright adhesive dots to the cat's body for decoration.

6 Stick adhesive dots to the top of the bottle cap to make the eyes and nose, draw pupils with the felt-tipped pen, and glue to the front of the body.

Television Set

Instead of watching the TV, why not make one from a cardboard box and appear on it yourself? Cover the box in kitchen foil, add an aerial and present your first show.

RECYCLING TIP
It takes quite a lot of kitchen foil to cover the TV so you could paint it with poster paints instead.

YOU WILL NEED
scissors or sharp knife (optional)
large cardboard box
pencil
ruler
kitchen foil
adhesive tape
paper in various shades
white glue
foil pie dish
2 knitting needles with
  rounded ends
3 bottle tops

paper

scissors

kitchen foil

foil pie dish

pencil

ruler

bottle tops

adhesive tape

glue

knitting needles

1 Carefully cut the flaps from the top of the cardboard box using a pair of scissors. Ask an adult to help you if the cardboard is very thick. They may need to use a knife.

2 Using a ruler, draw a large square on one side of the box and ask an adult to help you to cut it out. Leave enough room for the control panel on one side.

3 Cut lengths of kitchen foil. Loosely crumple the foil to make a crinkled surface and then tape the foil around the box until the outside is covered.

4 Cut a piece of bright paper large enough to cover the inside of the box opposite the opening. Glue it to the inside of the box to make a bright background.

5 Spread glue around the edge of the foil pie dish and stick it upside-down to the top of the TV. Glue the ends of the knitting needles into the top of the dish, to make the antennae of an aerial.

6 Cut a rectangle of bright paper and glue it to the space left for the control panel. Glue three bottle tops to the panel to make some control buttons.

Donkey Model

You will sometimes find an item that reminds you of something else, for example, an upside down old-fashioned clothes peg looks very like a donkey's head. The right way up, it makes a good leg, as the ends look like hooves. This little donkey is made from five wooden clothes pegs and a cardboard tube, and it looks very effective when painted.

YOU WILL NEED
cardboard tube
thin cardboard scraps
pencil
scissors
strong, non-toxic glue
5 old-fashioned wooden
  clothes pegs (pins)
elastic bands
corrugated cardboard scraps
purple, white and brown
  poster paints
paintbrushes
paint-mixing container

glue

cardboard tube

wooden pegs

scissors

poster paints

elastic band

pencil

paintbrush

1 Stand the end of the cardboard tube on a scrap piece of thin cardboard. Draw round it twice. Cut out the circles and glue one to each end of the tube.

2 Glue four pegs to the sides of the cardboard tube, two at each end, to make legs. Hold in place with elastic bands while the glue dries. This may take a few hours.

3 Cut a small strip of corrugated cardboard. Glue it to one end of the carboard tube and leave to dry completely. Glue a peg to the cardboard to make the head.

4 Once the glue has dried, paint the donkey purple. When the paint has dried, add white markings and the donkey's eyes. Paint its ears and hooves brown.

Pull-along Snake

This slithery snake is very simple to make from plastic bags, straws and a small yogurt pot. Plastic bags come in all sorts of bright shades; so, if you see a nice one, keep it.

YOU WILL NEED
scissors
green and yellow carrier bags
green and yellow drinking straws
thin cord in a bright shade
3 wooden beads
small yogurt pot
pencil
thin cardboard
darning needle
white glue
red plastic bag

wooden beads

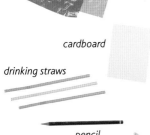

plastic bags

cardboard

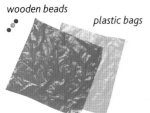

drinking straws

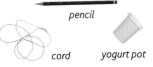

pencil

cord   *yogurt pot*

scissors   *glue*

1 Cut sections from the plastic bags. Cut circles of plastic from the bags. You will need about 15 of each shade. Fold each circle in four and snip the point to make a hole.

2 Cut 1cm (½in) pieces of yellow and green straws. You will need 20 of each. Cut a long length of cord and tie a knot in the end. Thread a bead on to the cord and then six pieces of straw. Thread on a green circle then a green straw, followed by a yellow circle and yellow straw. Repeat until you have used up all the pieces.

3 To make the head, cut the rim from a yogurt pot. Draw around the rim of the pot on to thin cardboard and cut out the shape. Ask an adult to help you to make a hole in the middle of the cardboard shape and the bottom of the pot.

4 Thread the cardboard on to the cord and then the pot. Glue the cardboard to the pot's rim. Tie a knot above the pot. Glue a forked tongue, cut from the red bag, to the bottom of the pot and two green beads to the top for the eyes.

Snake Sock-puppets

One good way to give your old socks a new lease of life is to make them into puppets. These snakes are decorated with bright felt. Once you've made a snake, why not make some other characters to keep it company?

YOU WILL NEED
felt scraps in various shades
scissors
white glue
1 sock

felt scraps

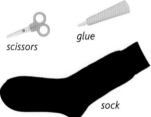

scissors *glue*

sock

1 To make the snake's eyes, cut two circles of felt. Cut two smaller circles of a different shade and glue them to the middle of the larger felt circles.

2 Glue the snake's eyes in position at the top of the sock.

3 Cut diamonds and strips of felt in various shades. Glue the strips at equal distances along the length of the sock. Glue the diamonds between the strips.

4 Cut a forked tongue from red felt. Glue the tongue to the top of the toe of the sock, in the middle. Allow the glue to dry thoroughly before you play with your sock puppet.

Wooden Spoon Puppets

You can make puppets from all sorts of things, but wooden spoons are especially good because they are just the right shape to make a head and a body. Gather a piece of fabric to hide the spoon handle, paint a face at the top and away you go!

YOU WILL NEED

wooden spoon
pink, blue, brown and yellow
  poster paints
paintbrush
paint-mixing container
pencil
ruler
fabric
scissors
darning needle
matching sewing thread
strong, non-toxic glue
satin ribbon scrap
gold and bright foil

paintbrush

poster paints

satin ribbon

fabric

pencil

scissors

bright foil

wooden spoon

sewing thread

glue

1 Paint the top half of the wooden spoon pink and leave it to dry completely. Draw the puppet's eyes, nose, mouth and hair in pencil on the spoon and then fill in its features using poster paints.

2 Cut a piece of fabric as long as the spoon handle and 30cm (12in) wide. Sew running stitches along the top edge of the fabric and pull the threads to gather the material. Knot the ends of the threads together.

3 Glue the gathered edge of the fabric around the spoon handle, below the puppet's face. Glue a short scrap of satin ribbon around the puppet's neck, to cover the top of the gathered fabric.

4 Cut a crown from gold foil and glue it to the top of the head. Cut two circles of bright foil and glue one to the middle of the crown and the other at the middle of the satin ribbon, as 'jewels'.

Pop-up Puppet

Make a pop-up puppet from an old wooden spoon and a plastic flowerpot. This puppet is a cat, but you can make all sorts of characters using the same basic instructions.

RECYCLING TIP
Ask permission before you raid the kitchen for wooden spoons.

YOU WILL NEED
ruler
orange felt
scissors
flowerpot
dressmaker's pins
darning needle
sewing thread
strong, non-toxic glue
orange, red and blue poster paint
medium and fine paintbrushes
paint-mixing container
long-handled wooden spoon
felt-tipped pen
small bell
thin cord in a bright shade
bright adhesive dots

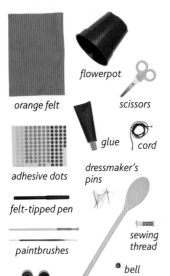

orange felt

flowerpot

scissors

glue

cord

adhesive dots

dressmaker's pins

felt-tipped pen

paintbrushes

sewing thread

bell

poster paints

wooden spoon

1 Cut a piece of felt measuring 20cm (8in) wide and long enough to fit around the inside of the flowerpot with 2cm (¾in) to spare.

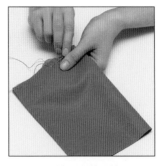

2 Fold the felt in half widthways. Pin the two shorter sides together. Sew the edges of the felt, using small running stitches. Sew a line of long running stitches along the long edge of the felt. Leave the threads long to gather up the fabric.

3 Glue the folded long edge of the felt around the inside of the flowerpot, with the edge to be gathered at the top.

4 Paint a long-handled wooden spoon orange. When dry, draw the cat's features with the felt-tipped pen, then paint them with the fine paintbrush. Cut two triangles of orange felt and glue them to the top to make the cat's ears.

5 Pass the handle through the hole in the bottom of the pot. Pull the threads in the top of the felt tight to gather it together, and knot the ends. Put a little glue around the top of the handle and stick the gathered edge of the felt to it.

6 Cut two arms from scraps of felt and glue one to each side of the cat's body. Put a small bell on a length of bright cord and tie it around the cat's neck. Decorate the rim of the flowerpot with a row of adhesive dots.

Glove Puppets

If you've lost one of a pair of gloves, why not make this funny puppet family and their pet bird? Their hair is made from scraps of bright fabric and their faces are little beads and other odds and ends. Once you have made this puppet, why not try adapting the design to make a range of different characters and stage a show using other puppets too.

YOU WILL NEED
thick blue and green thread
darning needle
1 glove
scissors
thin satin ribbon
fine felt-tipped pen
felt scraps
white glue
small beads and buttons

sewing thread

beads and buttons

thin satin ribbon

glove

scissors

felt scraps

1 To make the blue hair on the little finger, sew loops of blue thread into the top edge of the finger. Make a small stitch after each loop to keep it in place.

2 To make the braided hair, sew long loops of green thread into the top edge of the third finger. Make a small stitch after each loop to keep it in place.

3 Snip the ends of the green loops and trim the thread so that it is straight. Braid the pieces of thread and tie the end of the braid with the satin ribbon.

4 Draw the hair, bow-tie and all the other shapes required on scraps of bright felt, using the felt-tipped pen. Cut them out carefully.

5 Glue the felt shapes to the front of the fingers, using white glue. Leave to dry.

6 Arrange all the beads and other odds and ends on the puppets and glue them in place. Let the glue dry thoroughly before you play with your glove puppets.

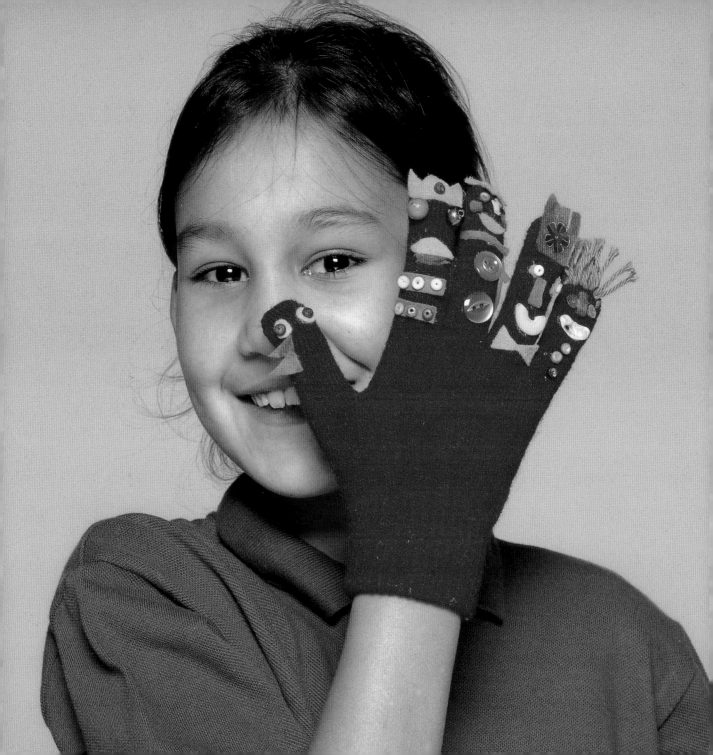

Pinball Table

Make this exciting pinball game and you'll have hours of fun! The bollards are made from small cotton reels and yogurt pots and the marble is kept on the table by elastic bands. Ask an adult to get you some strong, non-toxic glue, to stick the bollards to the table, otherwise the elastic bands will pull them off again.

TO PLAY PINBALL

The aim of the game is to keep the ball moving for as long as possible. Time how long it takes for it to reach the bottom of the table each time.

YOU WILL NEED

scissors
thin cardboard
red, yellow and blue
  poster paints
paint-mixing container
paintbrush
white glue
cotton reels (spools)
very strong, non-toxic glue
bright adhesive dots
3 small yogurt cartons
foam board, measuring
  90 x 60cm (36 x 24in)
pencil
thin paper in bright shades
long, thin, loose elastic bands
marble

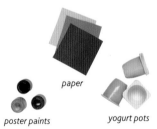

paper

poster paints

yogurt pots

marble

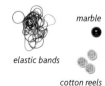

elastic bands

cotton reels

bright adhesive dots

1 Cut small circles of cardboard to cover the top of each cotton reel. Paint the cardboard circles in various bright shades. Leave the paint to dry completely.

2 Add a little white glue to some red poster paint. Paint the reels red and leave them to dry. Glue a brght circle to the top of each reel and stick a dot in the middle.

3 Carefully cut away most of the rims of the yogurt cartons, leaving a narrow, trimmed edge. This will prevent the marble from catching on the rims.

4 Mark the positions for the bollards on the board. Put two under the top corners, so the board slopes. Glue them all in place and leave to dry overnight.

5 Draw numbers, arrows and stars on scraps of bright paper. Carefully cut them all out and glue them to the table, as shown in the main picture opposite.

6 Stretch an elastic band between pairs of cotton reels, as shown, to link them all. Tie an elastic band between two bollards at the bottom to launch the marble.

Fruit Machine

Test your luck with this fun fruit machine. Each cotton reel has three symbols on it; spin them, and if they all show the same symbol award yourself a treat.

YOU WILL NEED

cardboard cereal box
small cardboard box
pencil
scissors
paper glue
red, yellow and green thin paper
knitting needle with a
   rounded end
3 large cotton reels (spools)
4 small cotton reels
cork
pink and green poster paints
paintbrush
paint-mixing container
confectionery

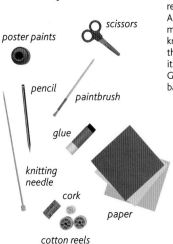

poster paints
scissors
pencil
paintbrush
glue
knitting needle
cork
paper
cotton reels

1 Open out the boxes and lay them flat. Draw three holes for the cotton reels on the front of the cereal box. Ask an adult to cut them out and make holes on the sides for the knitting needle. Draw a rectangle on the front of the smaller box and cut it out. Glue the boxes back together. Glue a rectangle of red paper to the back of the small box.

2 Cut three strips of paper in different shades, as wide as the large cotton reels and long enough to fit around them. Cut out a triangle, a square and a circle in each of the three shades too.

3 Glue the yellow square, circle and triangle to the green strip, the red shapes to the yellow strip and the green shapes to the red. Glue a strip around each large reel, to make the fruit machine's dials.

4 Thread the knitting needle through the hole in one side of the cereal box. Thread a small cotton reel on to the needle as a spacer; then a dial; then another spacer; then a dial, until all are in place and visible through the holes. Thread the end of the needle through the hole in the other side of the box.

5 Glue the smaller box to the front of the fruit machine to make the prize box. Ask an adult to help you to push a cork on to the end of the knitting needle to keep it in place.

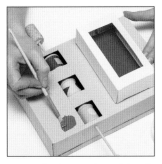

6 Paint the fruit machine pink and the prize box green. When the paint has dried completely, cut three small yellow stars and glue them to the top of the machine, above the holes. Fill the prize box with a selection of confectionery.

Catch-the-ball Game

Test your skill with this bat-and-ball game. It takes quite a lot of practice to catch the ball in the cup but it's good fun while you are learning! Use a plastic bottle with a long neck, because this makes a better handle to hold on to.

YOU WILL NEED
tissue paper sheets in
  bright shades
white glue
mixing container
clear plastic bottle
scissors
yogurt pot
strong, non-toxic glue
thin cord in a bright shade

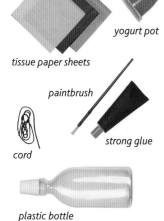

tissue paper sheets

yogurt pot

paintbrush

strong glue

cord

plastic bottle

1 Take two sheets of tissue paper in different shades and tear them into strips and circles.

2 Mix some white glue with a little water. Coat each strip of paper with glue. Cover the bottle with the paper. Add some circles of paper on top of the strips. Leave to dry thoroughly.

3 Carefully cut the corners from the top of the yogurt pot, leaving a very thin rim. Glue the pot to the middle of the bottle using strong glue. Leave to dry.

4 Roll a sheet of tissue paper tightly into a small ball. It should be small enough to fit inside the yogurt pot.

5 Cut a long piece of thin cord. Tie one end of the cord tightly around the ball of tissue paper.

6 Tie the other end of the thin cord securely around the end of the neck of the bottle.

Button Clacker

Button strings make a great clacking sound when you shake them against a cardboard tube. Collect old buttons and little beads as well, to make the strings look as interesting as possible. When you have finished, glue the plastic top back on to keep them in place.

YOU WILL NEED
orange, green and pink
  poster paints
paintbrushes
paint-mixing container
cardboard confectionery tube,
  with a lid
darning needle
thin cord in a bright shade
buttons and beads
strong, non-toxic glue

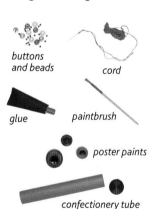

buttons
and beads

cord

glue

paintbrush

poster paints

confectionery tube

1 Paint the confectionery tube with orange and green stripes. When the paint is dry, add pink spots to the orange stripes.

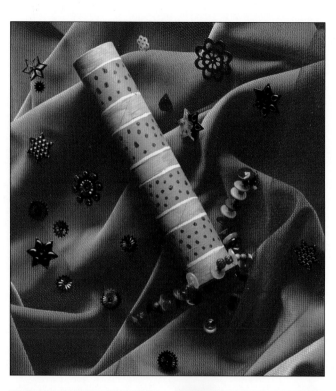

2 Thread a darning needle with some cord. Tie a knot in the end of the cord and thread on a button. Sew in and out of the button a few more times. Thread on beads and buttons, until you have a string about 12cm (5in) long, then make two more strings in the same way.

3 Ask an adult to make three holes in the top of the cardboard tube, leaving about 2.5cm (1in) between each hole. Then re-thread the needle with the end of one of the button strings.

4 Push the needle through one of the holes in the top of the tube, then back through the holes in the button. Tie the end tightly around the button. Attach the other two strings, then glue the lid back on.

Rhythm Sticks

Thin pieces of branch make great percussion sticks. Look out for two sticks that are about the same length and thickness next time you are in a park or wood. Make sure the branches are dry, so that they make a loud noise when you knock them together. If you wish, seal the surface of the sticks with non-toxic craft varnish after they have been painted.

YOU WILL NEED
2 sticks
white, red, green and yellow
   poster paints
paintbrush
paint-mixing container
scissors
string in a bright shade

string

scissors

poster paints

paintbrush

1 Remove any leaves and loose bark from the sticks and paint them white. Leave the sticks to dry.

2 Paint decorative red and green spots on top of the white paint. Make the spots different sizes.

3 When the spots have dried completely, fill in the white space between them with yellow paint. Leave a small white space around each dot, to highlight it and make it stand out.

4 Cut two long pieces of string. Tie one to the end of each stick. Wrap the string round and round the ends of the sticks to make handles. Tie the ends of the string very tightly so that they don't unravel.

Shaker

This shaker is filled with beads and buttons,
but you can use rice or dried beans.

YOU WILL NEED
clear plastic bottle, with cap
small beads and buttons
large and small bright
    adhesive dots
strong, non-toxic glue

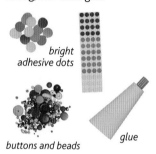

bright adhesive dots

buttons and beads

glue

1 Wash and dry the bottle. It should be dry inside as well. Pour a mixture of small beads and buttons into the bottle. A couple of handfuls will make a good noise.

2 Spread a line of glue around the inside of the bottle top. Screw the top on to the bottle. Stick adhesive dots to the outside to make a bright and decorative pattern.

3 Stick a row of small bright adhesive dots around the lower edge of the bottle top to make a pattern. Shake the instrument in time to music.

Tambourine

Two foil pie dishes can quickly and easily
become a shiny tambourine.

RECYCLING TIP
If you can't find any little bells you could use small metal washers instead.

YOU WILL NEED
ruler
thin satin ribbon
scissors
small bells
adhesive tape
2 foil pie dishes
strong, non-toxic glue

foil pie dishes

glue

adhesive tape

bells

1 Cut about ten 10cm (3in) lengths of ribbon and tie a bell to each piece of ribbon.

2 Tape the bells around the inside edge of one of the pie dishes, making sure you space them evenly.

3 Spread glue around the rim of the second dish. Glue the dishes together, rim to rim. Leave to dry.

Drum

Drums are good fun to play and this one is portable, so you can play it wherever you are. The drum is made from an old plastic ice-cream tub and the drumsticks are knitting needles, with a wooden bead on the end.

YOU WILL NEED
ice-cream tub, with lid
yellow poster paint
paintbrush
paint-mixing container
white glue
paper glue
scissors
paper in various shades
thick cord in various shades
dried rice
strong, non-toxic glue
2 large wooden beads
2 knitting needles

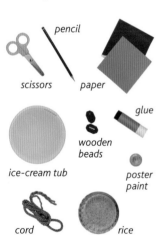

pencil

scissors   paper

glue

wooden
beads

ice-cream tub

poster
paint

cord   rice

1 Paint the outside of the ice-cream tub with bright poster paint mixed with a little white glue, so it sticks. When the paint is dry, cut out squares of red paper and glue them around the tub.

2 Ask an adult to punch a hole in both sides of the tub. Cut a length of thick cord in a bright shade and poke the ends through the holes in the tub. Tie a double knot in each end of the cord.

3 Put a handful of dried rice inside the tub and replace the lid on the container. You may need to tape it shut as it needs to be secure. The rice will make a swishing sound when you beat the drum.

4 Cut a circle of red paper to fit the top of the drum and glue it to the lid of the drum.

5 Cut diamonds of bright paper. Glue one on top of each square of paper around the sides of the drum and one to the top of the lid.

6 To make the drumsticks, use the strong glue to attach a large wooden bead to the end of each knitting needle. Leave the glue to dry thoroughly before you play your drum.

Groovy Guitar

Make yourself a groovy, twanging guitar from a cardboard tube and a large box. The strings are made from elastic bands and they rest on half a cardboard tube, which gives them quite loud different sounds.

RECYCLING TIP
You could cover the guitar with kitchen foil if you have some spare.

YOU WILL NEED
washing detergent box
felt-tipped pen
scissors or a sharp knife
long cardboard tube
brown-paper tape
cardboard tube
strong, non-toxic glue
yellow and orange poster paints
paintbrush
paint-mixing container
4 elastic bands
5 small cotton reels (spools)
kitchen foil
thick cord

brown-paper tape

cardboard tube

glue

kitchen foil

poster paints

paintbrush

1 Draw a square on the front of the washing detergent box. Ask an adult to help you to cut the square out of the box using scissors, or they could use a sharp knife.

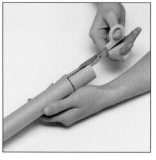

2 Draw a rectangle on one end of the cardboard tube. Ask an adult to help you cut the shape out of the tube, so that it will fit on the end of the box.

3 Put the tube on the end of the box as shown in the picture above, and tape it in place with brown-paper tape to make the neck of the guitar.

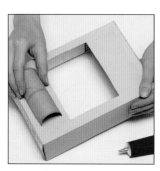

4 Cut a cardboard tube in half. Glue the half-tube below the hole in the front of the guitar.

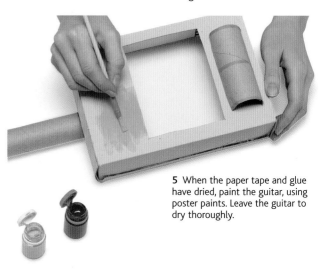

5 When the paper tape and glue have dried, paint the guitar, using poster paints. Leave the guitar to dry thoroughly.

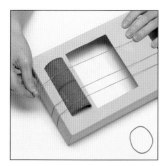

6 Stretch four elastic bands around the body of the guitar. Rest the elastic bands on the half cardboard, as this will make them louder when you play the guitar.

7 Cover five small cotton reels with kitchen foil, then glue four reels to the neck of the guitar to make pegs. Glue the other reel to the end of the guitar. Tie a length of cord from the neck of the guitar to the reel at the base of the guitar to make a strap.

Nail Chimes

Make beautiful music with these nifty nail chimes. They are suspended from a cardboard tube and, because they hang freely, they make a lovely, clear, ringing sound when you strike them. You will need to find bolts in various sizes, so that your chimes make different notes.

YOU WILL NEED
scissors
paper in various shades
cardboard tube
paper glue
bright adhesive dots
strong cord in a bright shade
bolts of various sizes
1 long bolt

paper

bolts

bright adhesive dots

cord

scissors

glue

cardboard tube

1 Cut a rectangle of paper as long as the cardboard tube and wide enough to fit around it. Stick the paper to the tube.

2 Stick a neat row of bright adhesive dots around each end of the cardboard tube, as shown, for decoration.

3 Cut a long length of strong cord, four times the length of the tube. It must be strong enough to bear the weight of all the bolts.

4 Make sure you leave a length of cord twice the length as the tube free, then tie the heads of each bolt to the second quarter of the length of cord. Make sure that the bolts are evenly spaced out and will hang along the length of the tube.

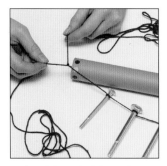

5 Thread the end of the cord you left free through the cardboard tube. Tie it to the other piece of cord securely, to form a loop that goes through the tube, with a long trailing end. The bolts should now be in the correct position.

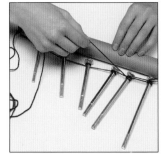

6 Loop the trailing length of cord two or three times around the head of each bolt again, then pass it back through the tube. Tie the ends tightly together. Hold the tube with one hand and play the chimes using the long bolt with the other hand.

Squeezy Bottle Dog Book-ends

These book-ends are made by covering two squeezy bottles with small pieces of papier-mâché and then painting them. The legs are made from corks and the ears and tails are cut from scraps of thin cardboard.

YOU WILL NEED
2 squeezy bottles
funnel
dried rice
masking tape
newspaper
white glue, diluted
8 corks
white, red, yellow, brown and
    black poster paints
paintbrushes
paint-mixing container
pencil
thin white cardboard
scissors

squeezy bottle

masking tape

rice   *corks*   *scissors*

glue

funnel

poster paints

paintbrushes

1 Wash and dry the squeezy bottles. Put a funnel in the top of each bottle and half-fill it with rice. Seal the top of each bottle with a strip of masking tape.

2 Tear the newspaper into strips. Dip each strip in the white glue and cover the bottles completely with two layers of paper. Leave the bottles to dry.

3 With white glue, stick four corks to one side of each squeezy bottle in order to make the legs. Leave the book-ends to dry thoroughly, preferably overnight.

4 Paint the dried book-ends white. You may have to use two coats of paint to cover up the newsprint completely. Leave the first coat to dry before adding a second.

5 Draw in the faces, collars and body markings with the pencil. Decorate the dogs using poster paints. You could copy the ones here, or make up your own design.

6 Draw four ears and two tails on the cardboard and cut out. Bend back the edges of each shape and glue ears and a tail on to each dog, using strong glue.

Nature Frame

This woody frame is made out of corrugated cardboard and covered with twigs and scraps of tree bark collected on a country walk. The frame has a 'spacer' in the middle, so you can push pictures into the frame from the top. You could glue fir cones on top of the twigs to make the frame even more decorative, if you like.

RECYCLING TIP
You could stick other natural items round the frame, such as feathers and little pebbles.

YOU WILL NEED
ruler
pencil
corrugated cardboard
scissors
strong, non-toxic glue
short twigs and pieces of bark

corrugated cardboard

scissors

glue

pencil

ruler

twigs and bark

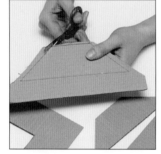

1 Measure out the frame pieces on corrugated cardboard, following the pattern at the front of the book. Cut out the pieces.

2 Glue the spacer piece to the frame back. You should make sure that the edges of the cardboard line up neatly.

3 Glue the front sections to the spacer to complete the frame. Leave to dry completely for about 10 minutes.

4 Glue the twigs and pieces of bark around the frame. Choose each piece of wood carefully, so that it naturally follows the shape of the frame. Add more than one layer of twigs for greater effect.

5 Cut out a stand for the frame on a piece of cardboard.

6 Make a fold in the long side of the stand. Spread a little strong glue along the fold and stick the stand to the middle of the back of the frame. Allow to dry before you use your frame.

Cardboard Frame

Corrugated cardboard is great for making frames, because it is strong and smooth and you can paint it easily. You can make your frame any size you want, so look for the large cardboard boxes used for electrical equipment.

YOU WILL NEED
ruler
pencil
thick corrugated cardboard
scissors
thin corrugated cardboard
strong, non-toxic glue
red, green, yellow and blue poster paints
paintbrush
paint-mixing container

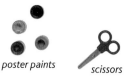

poster paints   *scissors*

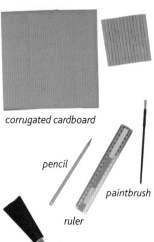

corrugated cardboard

pencil

paintbrush

ruler

glue

1 Measure and draw out the back of the frame and a spacer on a sheet of thick corrugated cardboard, following the pattern at the front of the book, then cut out the pieces using scissors.

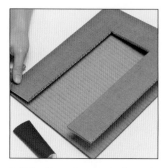

2 Using the pattern at the front of the book, draw out the pieces that make the front of the frame on thin cardboard. Cut them out. Glue the spacer to the frame back. Glue front pieces to the spacer.

3 Paint the frame using any bright poster paints. You may have to paint the frame twice to cover the cardboard completely. Allow the first coat of paint to dry before adding a second.

4 Cut circles and squares from the grooved side of a piece of thin corrugated cardboard.

5 Paint the corrugated cardboard shapes in bright shades.

6 When the paint is completely dry, glue the circles and squares around the frame to make a decorative border. Insert a picture of your choice and hang the frame on the wall or prop it up on a mantelpiece.

Papier-mâché Bowl

Papier-mâché is like magic because you can make all sorts of things from it, using only old newspapers and glue. This bowl is decorated by gluing bright strips of wrapping paper and paper shapes to its surface, and is good for holding fruit or odds and ends.

YOU WILL NEED
petroleum jelly
plastic bowl
newspaper
white glue, diluted
scissors
gift wrap
thin paper in various shades
white glue

glue   *newspaper*

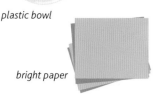

plastic bowl

bright paper

1 Grease your chosen bowl with a thin coating of petroleum jelly, so that the papier-mâché bowl will come out. Tear newspaper into 2.5cm (1in) wide strips. Dip the strips in the diluted white glue and press into the bowl, overlapping the edges slightly. Press in six layers and leave to dry overnight.

2 Gently pull the paper shape out of the bowl. Leave the papier-mâché bowl upside-down to dry. When it has dried, cut away the rough edges from the rim of the bowl.

3 Tear the gift wrap into strips and glue them to the outside and inside of the bowl to decorate it, overlapping the strips so no papier-mâché shows through.

4 Cut circles from the paper. Snip segments out of the paper to make stars.

5 Glue the stars to the middle and sides of the bowl, as shown in the picture here.

6 Cut lots of small squares from two shades of paper. Glue around the outside edge of the bowl.

Appliquéd Scarf

Wool blankets are lovely and warm, so if you find an old one that no one wants anymore, why not make it into a cosy scarf?

YOU WILL NEED

measuring tape
piece of thin wool blanket
scissors
orange, blue, green and pink felt
tracing paper
pencil
thin cardboard
felt-tipped pen
dressmaker's pins
darning needle
bright, thick sewing thread

wool blanket

thick sewing thread

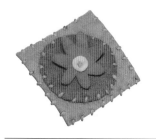

felt-tipped pen

felt

scissors

1 Cut a piece of blanket measuring about 60 x 90cm (24 x 36in). Fold it in half lengthways, so that the two long edges meet in the middle and overlap by 1.5cm (½in) on either side. Ask an adult to iron it, so the folds stay in place.

2 Cut six squares in total, 7 x 7cm (2½ x 2½in), from orange and blue felt. Then cut six circles to fit inside the squares from green and pink felt. Cut six much smaller circles from blue and yellow felt, to form the middles of the flowers.

3 Draw a flower pattern small enough to fit inside the felt circles on a piece of thin cardboard. Cut it out to make a template. Make six flowers by drawing around the template on scraps of felt. Cut them out.

4 Pin three squares to each end of the scarf and sew each square in place, using thick, bright thread. Sew a large circle on top of each square. Place a flower and small circle in the middle of each circle, and sew them in place with a few small stitches.

5 Fold the scarf so the flowers are on the inside. Pin the long edges together and sew them, using small running stitches. Place the scarf flat with the seam down the middle. Pin the top and bottom edges together. Sew along the top edge and halfway along the bottom.

6 Turn the scarf the right way out. Turn the rest of the lower edges to the inside of the scarf. Carefully sew the edges together, using small stitches. Ask an adult to iron the seams flat for you. This scarf cannot go in the washing machine, and should be hand-washed with care.

Pom-pom Hat

Beat the cold with this fun pom-pom hat. It's made by cutting down an old pair of wool tights. Leftover balls of wool are used to make two pom-poms to decorate the top of the hat and it looks so stylish that no one will be able to guess what it is made from.

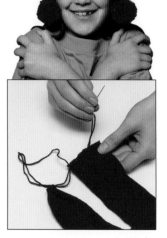

YOU WILL NEED
measuring tape
pair of wool tights
scissors
darning needle
thin wool (yarn)
pencil
pair of compasses
thin cardboard
knitting-wool oddments

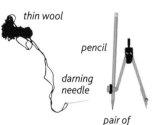
wool tights

scissors

thin wool

pencil

darning needle

pair of compasses

1 Measure 15cm (6in) down from the top of each leg of the tights. Cut off the legs at this point and discard them.

2 Thread the needle with the wool. Sew across the top of the cut ends, using small running stitches. Pull the stitching tight. Sew two more stitches to keep the ends gathered. Cut the thread.

3 Draw two identical circles with the pencil and a pair of compasses on the cardboard. Draw smaller circles inside. Cut out the larger ones. Ask an adult to help you to cut out the smaller ones.

4 Place the circles together. Tie the end of a length of wool around the circles. Wrap the wool around and around the circles, passing it through the central hole, until the hole is filled in.

5 Snip through the wool at the edge of the circles. Pull the circles slightly apart and tie a short piece of wool around the middle of the wool between the circles. Pull the circles off and trim any uneven wool.

6 Make a second pom-pom, then sew one to the end of each gathered leg. Roll up the waistband a couple of times to make a brim, and tie the legs loosely together in order to wear the hat.

Storage Chest

This small storage chest is great for keeping little treasures safe. It is made from large, empty matchboxes and is covered with scraps of plastic. You can make the chest as large as you want – just keep adding more matchboxes. You can also use large and small matchboxes, so you have lots of different-sized compartments.

RECYCLING TIP

This is an ideal storage place for those buttons, beads, pins and odds and ends that all good recyclers collect and keep.

YOU WILL NEED
green and red sticky-backed
  plastic (contact paper)
scissors
6 large matchboxes
strong, non-toxic glue
tracing paper
pencil
thin cardboard
6 plastic beads in bright shades

matchboxes

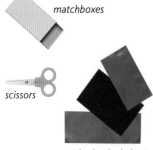
scissors

sticky-backed plastic

glue   *pencil*

plastic beads

1 Cut three green and three red pieces of sticky-backed plastic the same width and long enough to fit around a matchbox, and stick them on.

2 Cut six thin strips of red and six of green sticky-backed plastic. Stick them to the front and back of the box trays; red in green boxes and green in red boxes.

3 Spread strong glue along the long side of one green box and glue it to the side of a red box, and repeat with the other matchboxes so that you have three pairs.

4 When the glue has dried, glue the three pairs of boxes on top of each other to make the storage chest. Make sure that the edges of the boxes line up.

5 Carefully trace the pattern for the decoration; lay it face-down on a piece of cardboard; draw over the lines to transfer and cut it out. Cover the cardboard with sticky-backed plastic and trim.

6 Cut out a small red heart and stick it to the front of the decoration. Bend back the decoration's base and glue it to the top of the chest. Glue a plastic bead to the front of each tray for handles.

Printed Stationery

Personal stationery is often very expensive, but you can make your own by decorating it with these simple printing blocks. The pad of each block is made from shapes cut from washing-up sponges. Once you are used to the technique, make some blocks with your initials on.

YOU WILL NEED
pencil
ruler
thick corrugated cardboard
scissors
strong, non-toxic glue
felt-tipped pen
washing-up sponge
poster paints
paintbrush (optional)
saucer
writing paper

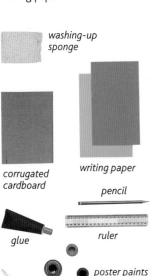

washing-up sponge

corrugated cardboard

writing paper

pencil

glue

ruler

poster paints

scissors

1 Carefully draw three 5 x 5cm (2 x 2in) squares and three 4 x 4cm (1½ x 1½in) squares on the corrugated cardboard, using a pencil and ruler. Cut out all the squares.

2 Glue the small squares upright on top of the larger squares to make printing blocks (the small squares are the handles for holding and using the blocks).

3 With a felt-tipped pen, draw simple shapes on to the washing-up sponge. Cut out the shapes and glue one to each printing block.

4 When the glue has dried, spread a little thick paint on a saucer. Dip a block into the paint or use the brush to coat it, so that the sponge is coated, and then press the block firmly on to a piece of writing paper to print the shape.

Patchwork Pencil Case

This bright pencil case is made in a patchwork design and will be the envy of all your friends at school. Patchwork is a great way to use up small scraps of pretty fabric.

YOU WILL NEED
pencil
ruler
thin cardboard scraps
scissors
felt scraps
felt-tipped pen
darning needle
bright sewing thread
dressmaker's pins
press studs (snap fasteners)
8 buttons

sewing thread

press studs

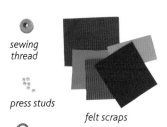
felt scraps

scissors

felt-tipped pen

buttons

pencil

1 Draw a square measuring 6 x 6cm (2½ x 2½in) on thin cardboard. Cut out the square to make a template. Draw round the template on to 16 scraps of felt.

2 Place the edges of two felt squares together. Sew the squares together with bright thread, using small running stitches. Sew on two more squares to make a row of four squares. Make another three rows of four felt squares. Place the four rows together and join with small running stitches to make a patchwork square.

3 Fold the top and bottom edges of the patchwork over. Sew along the folded edges, using small running stitches. Fold the patchwork square in half lengthways. Pin and sew the sides together. Sew press studs along the opening in the top of the pencil case.

4 Cut small squares from the leftover felt and sew a button to the middle of each one, then sew one to the middle of each square on the front of the case.

Jar Lid Badges

*Next time you finish a jar of jam, keep the lid to make a fun
badge. Cover the lids in kitchen foil and then cut shapes from
scraps of bright foil, saved from confectionery wrappers.
You can buy special badge pins but a safety pin is fine.*

YOU WILL NEED
scissors
kitchen foil
strong, non-toxic glue
jar lid
bright foil scraps
safety pin
adhesive tape

safety pin

adhesive tape

foil scraps

jar lid

kitchen foil

scissors

glue

1 Cut a square of foil that is about
4cm (1½in) larger all the way round
than the jam jar lid. Spread glue on
the back of the lid and then wrap it
in the foil. Squash the foil down on
the inside of the lid.

2 Cut a circle of gold foil and glue
it to the inside of the lid. Cut shapes
from scraps of bright foil and glue
them on top of the gold circle in an
interesting pattern.

3 As a change, you could snip the
edges of the gold foil circle to make
a 'star'.

4 Turn the badge over and put a
safety pin in the middle. Tape the
pin in place to make a fastener.

Squeezy-bottle Bracelets

Sections of a squeezy bottle are perfect for making bracelets and bangles, and you can decorate them in lots of different ways. Scraps of bright foil saved from confectionery wrappers make really cheerful stripes and you can also roll the foil to make glittery fake jewels.

YOU WILL NEED
squeezy bottle
scissors
adhesive tape
kitchen foil
bright foil scraps
strong, non-toxic glue

kitchen foil

scissors

foil scraps

glue

squeezy bottle

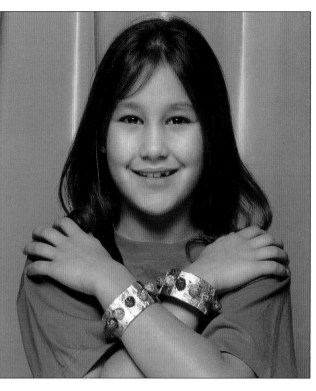

1 Wash and dry an empty squeezy bottle. Ask an adult to help you to cut a 2.5cm (1in) wide section from the bottle that is long enough to go round your wrist. Join the ends of the section together, using adhesive tape, to make a bangle.

2 Cut a piece of kitchen foil about twice the width of the bangle. Place the bangle on the foil and neatly press the foil around the bangle to cover it completely.

3 Smooth the scraps of foil with your fingers. Cut several strips of foil long enough to fit around the bangle. Glue the strips around the bangle at equal distances.

4 Roll more scraps of different foil into small beads and glue them around the outside of the bangle to make 'jewels'. Leave to dry before wearing your bracelets.

Rolled-paper Beads

Gift wrap comes in lovely designs and can be used in lots of different ways once you have finished unwrapping your presents! Bright paper makes wonderful beads, if you roll it around a pencil. Ask your family and friends to save all their scraps for you, and make an exciting and vibrant necklace.

YOU WILL NEED
ruler
pencil
gift wrap
scissors
paper glue
thin elastic

pencil

ruler

glue

scissors

1 Draw lots of 2.5cm (1in) wide strips on the back of a sheet of gift wrap. Make a mark halfway along one short edge of each strip. Draw lines from the two opposite corners to the marked point, dividing the strip into long, thin triangles.

gift wrap

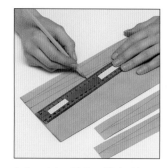

2 Cut along the lines on each strip to create neat triangles.

3 Starting at the bottom of the triangle, roll the strips of paper around a pencil. Roll them carefully, so the bead is even and the edges are neat. Put a little glue on the end of the paper.

4 Wrap the end over the bead and press it down. Leave the bead on the pencil until the glue is dry. When you have enough beads, thread them on to a length of elastic and knot the ends.

Foil-bead Pendant

Kitchen foil makes great adornments. You can roll it into little balls to make sparkling 'jewels', or make long, thin beads such as these, which are rolled around a pencil. A paper fastener taped to the back of the pendant makes a handy hanger to suspend the beads from.

YOU WILL NEED
ruler
pencil
kitchen foil
scissors
thin cardboard
strong, non-toxic glue
bright foil
sequins
gold adhesive star
adhesive tape
paper clip (fastener)
thin cord in a bright shade

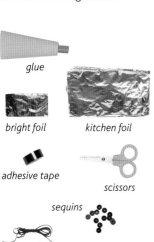

glue

bright foil   *kitchen foil*

adhesive tape

scissors

sequins

cord

pencil

1 Cut rectangles of foil measuring 30cm (12in) long and 2.5cm (1in) wide. Roll each strip around a pencil to make a bead. Glue the edges together. You will need about 20 beads altogether.

2 Draw a circle on a piece of thin cardboard, by drawing round the base of a jar or glass or using a pair of compasses. Cut out the circle and glue bright foil to each side of it to make the pendant.

3 Glue sequins in various shades around the edge of the pendant. Add a gold adhesive star to the middle of the circle. Tape a paper clip to the back of the pendant to make a hanger.

4 Cut a foil strip 20 x 2.5cm (8 x 1in); fold in half lengthways and in half again; glue the edges. Cut into 2.5cm (1in) lengths. Glue to the lower edge of the pendant's back. Thread the beads and pendant on to the cord.

Sponge-flower Headband

Washing-up sponges come in such pretty shades that it seems a pity not to use them in new ways. Here, pink, yellow and green sponges have been used to make a flower to decorate and brighten up a plain headband.

YOU WILL NEED
tracing paper
pencil
thin cardboard
scissors
yellow, pink and green
   washing-up sponges
thin black felt-tipped pen
darning needle
yellow, pink and green or
   blue threads
headband

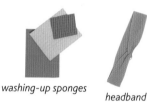

washing-up sponges

headband

sewing thread

scissors

felt-tipped pen

1 Carefully trace the flower patterns from the front of the book. Lay the tracings, face-down, on the cardboard and draw over the lines again. Cut out the shapes to make a template.

2 Place the flower template on the yellow sponge, the flower middle on the pink sponge and the leaf template on the green sponge. Draw around the templates using the felt-tipped pen and then cut out the shapes.

3 Place the pink flower middle in the middle of the flower. Sew the middle to the flower with three or four small stitches, using pink thread so they don't show up too much.

4 Place the leaves, pointing outwards, on the front of the headband. Sew on the stems with blue or green thread. Lay the flower on top of the stems, and sew its middle and edges to the band with yellow thread.

Nature Box

If you go for a walk in the countryside or a park you will probably find twigs, seed pods, fir cones and so on, which make lovely decorations. This plain cardboard box has been painted green and then rows of acorns, seed pods and small and large fir cones have been added to make it really decorative. Always ask an adult to look at what you have found to see that it is safe before you use it. Carefully wash everything before you position it.

YOU WILL NEED
green poster paint
paintbrush
paint-mixing container
cardboard box, with lid
acorns, fir cones and seed pods
strong, non-toxic glue

 acorns

 small fir cones   glue

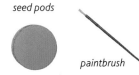 seed pods   poster paint

cardboard box   paintbrush

1 Paint the lid and base of the cardboard box with poster paint and leave it to dry thoroughly.

2 Arrange a row of acorns around the edge of the lid of the box, as shown, and glue them in position. Try to be as neat as possible.

3 Glue a large fir cone to the middle of the lid. Glue small fir cones to the top of the lid, between the acorns and the large fir cone.

4 Glue a row of seed pods at equal distances around the sides of the box. Let the glue dry thoroughly before you use your box.

Fabric Scrap Picture

Raid the sewing basket to find scraps of fabric to make a picture. You will need a fairly large piece of material to make the background and smaller pieces to make the hen and the trees. If you don't have any fabric glue, use white glue instead.

YOU WILL NEED
ruler
cardboard in a bright shade
scissors
fabric scraps
tracing paper
pencil
thin cardboard
thin black felt-tipped pen
fabric or white glue

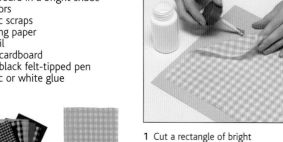

fabric

ruler

pencil

glue

scissors

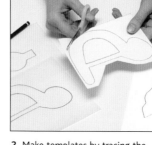

1 Cut a rectangle of bright cardboard measuring 25 x 30cm (10 x 12in). Cut a piece of fabric measuring 23 x 28cm (9 x 11in). Glue together.

2 Make templates by tracing the patterns for this project from the front of the book on to thin cardboard with a felt-tipped pen. Cut them out.

3 Draw around the tree template on two scraps of green fabric, using a thin black felt-tipped pen. Cut out the trees and glue one to each end of the picture.

4 Put the chicken template on blue fabric and the wing on blue checked fabric. Draw around them, using the felt-tipped pen and cut them out carefully using scissors. Glue the chicken's body to the middle of the picture. Glue its wing on top of its body.

5 Carefully cut the chicken's legs, face and feet from scraps of fabric and glue them in place. Cut long, wavy strips of red fabric to make the patterns on the trees, and glue them in place.

6 Glue a strip of green checked fabric to the bottom of the picture for grass, and a strip of blue checked fabric to the top for the sky. Cut a circle of red checked fabric for the sun and use small scraps of red fabric for its rays. Leave the picture to dry before displaying it.

Straw Mobile

Drinking straws come in wonderful bright shades and you can use them to make lots of different projects. This mobile is made from pieces of straw threaded together.

YOU WILL NEED
scissors
drinking straws in various shades
ruler
cotton cord in a bright shade
strong, non-toxic glue
large buttons
wooden beads

drinking straws

beads

scissors

buttons

cord

glue

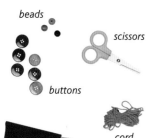

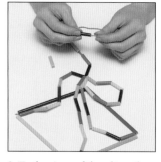

1 Cut four different straws into 12cm (4in) pieces. Cut a long piece of cord and thread the straw pieces on to it. Tie the ends of the cord, so that the straws make a square.

2 Cut more straws into 2.5cm (1in) lengths. Tie a length of bright cord at each corner of the straw square. Thread the pieces of straw on to the thread.

3 Tie the pieces of thread together at the top. Tie another length of cord to the top of the mobile and thread some more short lengths of straw on to it.

4 Cut four 2.5cm (1in) pieces and one 5cm (2in) piece of straw in the same shade. Glue the longer piece of straw to the back of a large button. Glue two short pieces of straw on each side of the long piece. Glue another button on top to make a star. Make four more stars in different shades.

5 Cut four different lengths of bright cord and tie one to each corner of the square, so that they hang down. Cut 2.5cm (1in) lengths of straw and thread them on to the cord, changing the shade of the straw each time. Thread a star on to the end of each cord and one on the top of the mobile.

6 Thread a wooden bead on the end of each piece of cord, to keep the stars in place. Securely knot the ends of the four cords that hang down and trim the ends so they are neat. Leave a long cord at the top of the mobile to make a hanger. Suspend the mobile from a hook on the ceiling.

Pine Cone Mobile

Pine cones are lovely objects and they look great suspended from a mobile. The bars of this mobile are made from lengths of twig and the pine cones are tied at different heights. Pine cones are very much a part of winter, and you could paint your twigs and cones with gold or silver poster paint to make a Christmas mobile.

YOU WILL NEED
scissors
thin cord
pine cones
2 thin twigs and 1 forked twig

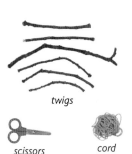

twigs

scissors   *cord*

1 Cut lengths of cord and attach each one to the top of a pine cone. Tie a pine cone to both ends of two short twigs.

2 Tie the two twigs together with the cord, one above the other, to make the mobile shape.

3 Tie more small pine cones to the lower section of the mobile. Hang them at different heights so they make an attractive shape once the mobile is hung up.

4 Tie a large forked twig to the upper twig. Wrap the two together tightly by winding cord around them. Tie a length of cord to the top of the mobile to make a hanger.

Felt-scrap Christmas Cards

There are always lots of leftover scraps when you make something out of felt. Its a pity to waste them, even if they're quite small, because you can use them to make bright greetings cards. Save scraps of vivid paper and cardboard, as well, to make backings for the cards.

YOU WILL NEED
pencil
ruler
thin cardboard in a bright shade
scissors
fine felt-tipped pen
scraps of bright felt
white glue

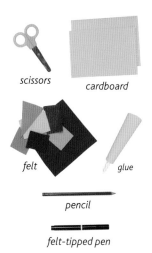

scissors

cardboard

felt

glue

pencil

felt-tipped pen

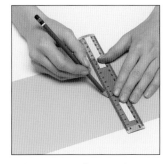

1 Draw a rectangle measuring 22 x 15cm (9 x 6in) on the cardboard. Cut out the rectangle and fold it in half.

2 Draw a tree shape on a scrap of green felt and a tub on a piece of pink felt, using the fine felt-tipped pen. Cut out the shapes carefully using scissors.

3 Cut a rectangle of blue felt slightly smaller than the cardboard backing. Glue the tree and the tub to the blue felt.

4 Glue the picture to the front of the cardboard. Cut small circles of felt to make baubles and glue them to the tree.

Paper-clip Christmas Decorations

These shiny Christmas decorations will add a sparkle to your Christmas tree. Decorate them with scraps of bright foil from confectionery wrappers, and sandwich clips between them to make the decorations look like icicles.

YOU WILL NEED
pencil
pair of compasses
thin cardboard
scissors
kitchen foil
bright foil
strong, non-toxic glue
silver paper clips (fasteners)
thin silver elastic

glue

paper clips

bright foil

silver elastic

kitchen foil

scissors

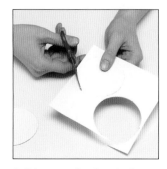

1 Using a pencil and a pair of compasses, draw two circles exactly the same size on the cardboard, and then cut them out.

2 Cut two squares of kitchen foil about 4cm (1½in) bigger all the way around than the circles of cardboard. Place a cardboard circle in the middle of each piece of foil. Wrap the edges of the foil over the cardboard circle.

3 Cut a circle of bright foil and snip small triangles from its edges to make a 'star' shape. Glue to the front of one of the cardboard circles. Cut two circles from bright foil and glue them to the middle of the star.

4 Glue a row of paper clips to the back of the other covered circle. Glue the two circles together. Tie a length of thin silver elastic to the top of the decoration to make a hanger and suspend it.

Pasta-shape Christmas Tree Decorations

These Christmas-tree decorations are made from plastic dessert cartons. They are painted in bright shades and then decorated with pieces of dried pasta, which comes in lots of lovely shapes and sizes. Mix the paint with white glue first, so that it sticks to the plastic.

YOU WILL NEED
2 plastic dessert cartons
white glue
green, gold and pink poster paints
paintbrush
dried pasta shapes
2 gold pipe cleaners
strong, non-toxic glue

glue

poster paint

paintbrush

gold pipe cleaners

dried pasta shapes

1 Wash and dry the cartons. Mix a little glue with green poster paint and paint one carton. Repeat with pink paint and the second carton. When dry, paint the top and bottom edges gold.

2 Paint the pasta shapes you have chosen with gold poster paint. Leave them to dry thoroughly.

3 Ask an adult to help you to make a hole in the top of the cartons. Push both ends of the pipe cleaners through the holes. On the inside of the dishes, bend the ends of the pipe cleaners outwards to keep them in place.

4 Spread a little glue around the edge of each pasta shape. Glue the shapes around the sides of the cartons. Thread a pasta shape over the top of each pipe cleaner and glue them to the top of the decoration. Leave to dry.

Christmas Door Hanging

This cheerful door decoration is easy to make from foil pie dishes and clothes pegs. Kitchen foil always looks Christmassy and the smiling snowman will brighten up any door or window.

VARIATION
Any picture could go in the middle of the hanging – try a gold star or a jolly Santa Claus.

YOU WILL NEED
pencil
thin bright and white paper
scissors
paper glue
7 small foil pie dishes
strong, non-toxic glue
7 plastic clothes pegs (pins)
large foil pie dish
bright ribbon
adhesive tape

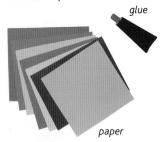
glue

paper

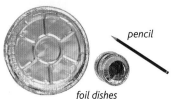
pencil

foil dishes

ribbon

scissors

clothes pegs

1 Draw circles the same size as the bottoms of the small pie dishes on the paper and cut them out.

2 With paper glue, stick the paper circles to the middles of the small pie dishes. Cut stars from scraps of the paper and glue one to the middle of each circle.

3 Using the strong glue, stick each of the small pie dishes to the top of a plastic clothes peg.

4 Draw and cut out a large circle of bright paper to cover the bottom of the large dish. Glue it in place.

5 Cut a snowman from white paper and glue him to the middle of the large pie dish. Cut his hat, face, arms and buttons from scraps of bright paper and glue them in place.

6 Clip the small pie dishes around the larger one, using the clothes pegs. Tape a piece of bright ribbon to the back of the large pie dish to make a hanger.

INDEX

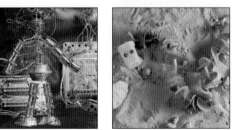